MEALS IN A JAR COOKBOOK

The Ultimate Guide with Quick and Easy Homemade tasty Recipes in Jars.

KAREN ALBRECHT

Copyright @ 2023 by Karen Albrecht

All rights reserved. No part of this publication may be reproduced, distributed, or transmitted in any form or by any means, including photocopying, recording, or other electronic or mechanical methods, without the prior written permission of the publisher, except in the case of brief quotations embodied in critical reviews and certain other noncommercial uses permitted by copyright law.

OTHER BOOKS BY KAREN ALBRECHT

Freeze-Drying Cookbook

https://getbook.@/freezedryingbyKaren

Pressure Canning

https://getbook.@/Canning byKaren

Dehydrator cookbook

https://getbook.@/DehydratorbyKaren

TABLE OF CONTENTS

INTRODUCTION	**7**
CHAPTER 1: WHY MEALS IN A JAR?	**11**
The Art and Science of Meals in a Jar: An Extensive Aide	11
Benefits of Meal Prepping in Jars	15
Choosing the Right Jars and Equipment	19
Chapter 2: Breakfast Recipes in a jar	**23**
Classic Overnight Oats	23
Berry Blast Parfait	24
Veggie and Cheddar Omelet Jar	25
Chia Pudding Delight	25
Mediterranean Quinoa Bowl	26
Pesto and Tomato Breakfast Jar	27
Spinach and Feta Breakfast Jar	27
Banana Nut Overnight Oats	28
Avocado and Egg Breakfast Jar	29
Peanut Butter and Banana Chia Pudding	30
Chapter 3: Snacks and Sweets in Jars	**31**
Trail Blend Energy Chomps	31
Layered Greek Yogurt Parfait	32
Apple Cinnamon Biscuit Jar	33
No-Heat Chocolate Cheesecake	34
Mango Coconut Chia Pudding	35

Chocolate Peanut Butter Delight	35
Lemon Blueberry Cheesecake Parfait	36
Almond Satisfaction Chia Pudding	36
Caramel Fruity dessert Short-term Oats	37
Banana Split Breakfast Jar	38
Chapter 4: Main course mix in a jar	**39**
Mexican Enchilada Goulash	39
Baked Ziti with Sausage	40
Yam and Dark Bean Bake	41
Chicken and Broccoli Alfredo	42
Eggplant Parmesan	42
Teriyaki Salmon with Brown Rice	43
Spinach and Feta Stuffed Ringer Peppers	44
Lemon Garlic Shrimp and Orzo	45
Pesto Chicken with Sun-Dried Tomatoes	45
Meat and Grain Stew	46
Chapter 5: Soup and sauce mix in a jar	**47**
Classic Tomato Soup	47
Rich Mushroom Sauce	48
Zesty Lentil Soup	49
Velvety Garlic Parmesan Sauce	49
Moroccan Chickpea Soup	50
Smooth Alfredo Sauce	51
Thai Coconut Curry Soup	51
Rich Wild Mushroom Sauce	52
Part Pea and Ham Soup	53

Sun-Dried Tomato Pesto Sauce	53
Chapter 6: Rice mix in a jar	**55**
Mexican Rice Mix	55
Lemon Spice Rice Mix	56
Coconut Curry Rice Mix	57
Spanish Rice Mix	57
Herbed Wild Rice Mix	58
Garlic Parmesan Rice Mix	59
Thai Pineapple Broiled Rice Mix	59
Mushroom Risotto Mix	60
Lemon Asparagus Rice Mix	61
Mediterranean Couscous Mix	61
Chapter 7: Expert Tips for Storing and Reheating Meals	**63**
Customizing Recipes to Suit Your Tastes	66
CONCLUSION	**69**

INTRODUCTION

In the clamoring city of Serenityville, Emily was known for her vast energy and tight timetable. Adjusting a requesting position and her enthusiasm for climbing allowed for intricate feasts. That is the point at which she found the enchantment of dinner preparing in Jars. Furnished with a heap of bricklayer containers and a variety of new ingredients, Emily set out on a culinary experience.

She painstakingly layered energetic vegetables, protein-pressed grains, and delightful sauces, making an ensemble of varieties and surfaces in each jar.

Monday mornings were currently a breeze. Emily just snatched a container loaded up with for the time being oats, finished off with a mixture of berries, nuts, and a touch of honey. It was a great explosion of energy to launch her week. As the days passed, Emily's dinners developed significantly more imaginative. Thai-roused noodle servings of mixed greens hit the dance floor with cilantro, peanuts, and a fiery nut dressing.

Good stews with delicate lumps of meat and a sweet-smelling mix of flavors warmed her spirit during cold nights. Her partners wondered about her scrumptious and perfectly introduced snacks. Inquisitive about her mysterious, Emily facilitated an end of the week studio, showing them the specialty of feast preparing in containers. Together, they diced, layered, and fixed containers loaded up with delicious manifestations.

Word spread like quickly, and soon, the whole office was in on Emily's culinary mystery. Serenityville started to buzz with the smell of newly made feasts in containers, and a recently discovered feeling of wellbeing and imperativeness pervaded the city. Emily's energy didn't stop at appetizing dishes. She created flavorful treats as well.

Layers of velvety yogurt, crunchy granola, and delicious organic products made for a virtuous extravagance that fulfilled even the best tooth.

Through her commitment and imagination, Emily had changed her own life as well as a whole local area's way to deal with sustenance. Serenityville turned into a city known for its solid and delightful jostled dinners, and Emily's kitchen studios turned into a loved practice.

Emily's story spread all over, moving others to assume responsibility for their own sustenance. Her heritage lived on in each container of goodness, a demonstration of the force of assurance and a little imagination in the kitchen.

Thus, in the core of Serenityville, the fragrance of bumped culinary victories consumed the space, an update that with a touch of planning and creativity, anybody could enjoy the flavor of an even life.

CHAPTER 1: WHY MEALS IN A JAR?

The Art and Science of Meals in a Jar: An Extensive Aide

In the cutting edge tornado of life, finding a harmony between a feverish timetable and a craving for healthy, delightful dinners can be a test. Enter the shrewd idea of "Meals in a Jar." This imaginative way to deal with dinner planning offers a large group of advantages that reform the manner in which we eat, joining comfort, sustenance, and culinary innovation in a solitary bundle.

1. Proficiency and Comfort:
Smoothed out Dinner Planning: Dinners in a Container smooth out the cooking system. By gathering fixings ahead of time, you save valuable time during the week.

In and out Arrangements: For occupied experts, understudies, or anybody with a high speed way of life, a pre-stuffed container offers a helpful, convenient feast choice.

2. Conservation of Freshness:
Expanded Time span of usability: The water/air proof mark of a container safeguards the newness and kinds of ingredients, decreasing food waste and it is basically as superb as the first to guarantee each nibble.

Deterrent Estimates Against Deterioration: The container goes about as a boundary, protecting against outside impurities and keeping up with the nature of the dinner.

3. Nourishing Respectability:
Adjusted Nourishment: Feasts in a Container empower exact part control, working with adjusted and segment proper servings of proteins, grains, vegetables, and the sky's the limit from there.

Protection of Supplements: With ingredients layered in a calculated way, every part holds its healthy benefit, advancing a better eating routine.

4. Various Culinary Open doors:
Artistic liberty: The jar fills in as a material for culinary masterfulness, considering a variety of imaginative mixes and flavor profiles.
Worldwide Cooking Experiences: Investigate the world's cooking styles by layering different ingredients, from Mediterranean grains to Asian-roused noodle bowls.

5. Supportability and Naturally Cognizant Decisions:
Diminished Bundling Waste: Using reusable jars limits the requirement for expendable compartments, adding to a more economical way of life.
Accentuation on New, Entire ingredients: Dinner preparing in containers empowers the utilization of entire, natural food varieties, advancing reasonable rural practices.

6. Wellbeing and Health:

Careful Eating: The purposeful course of layering ingredients energizes careful thought of every part's dietary benefit, cultivating better dietary patterns.

Controlled Bits: Segment control helps with weight the board and supports a decent way to deal with calorie consumption.

7. Local area and Sharing:

Social Viewpoint: Dinner preparing in a jar can be a collective action, cultivating a feeling of brotherhood and shared liability regarding wellbeing and prosperity.

Motivation and Recipe Trade: The developing ubiquity of Dinners in a Container has prompted a lively web-based local area, where fans share recipes, tips, and imaginative thoughts.

All in all, Meals in a jar rise above the domain of simple comfort food. They address a comprehensive way to deal with nourishment, proficiency, and culinary articulation. By taking on this creative technique, people can enjoy the advantages of adjusted, delightful dinners while at the same time adding to a more economical, wellbeing cognizant way of life.

Benefits of Meal Prepping in Jars

In the present quick moving world, carving out the opportunity to plan healthy, nutritious feasts can be an overwhelming undertaking. Enter the extraordinary act of Meals Prepping in a jar. This inventive way to deal with dinner readiness offers a huge number of benefits that smooth out the cooking system as well as advance better, more careful dietary patterns. In this part, we will dig into the many advantages of this culinary transformation, showing the way that it can alter your way to deal with sustenance and using time effectively.

1. Efficiency and Time-Saving:

Advanced Planning Time: Dinner preparing in containers considers productive grouping of ingredients, fundamentally lessening the time spent on day to day feast gathering.

Smoothed out Cooking Cycle: With pre-estimated and prepared ingredients, cooking turns into a consistent encounter, killing the requirement for somewhat late basic food item runs or broad prep work.

2. Segment Control and Adjusted Nourishment:

Accuracy in Dividing: Jars offer a reasonable visual aide for segment sizes, advancing adjusted sustenance and assisting with keeping away from overindulgence.

Fluctuated Ingredient Layering: The container design supports smart layering of proteins, grains, vegetables, and sauces, guaranteeing an amicable mix of supplements in every feast.

3. Protection of Freshness and Flavor:

Impermeable Seal: Jars give an immaculate seal, shielding the honesty of every ingredient and protecting the newness of the dinner.

Improved Taste Insight: With flavors and surfaces saved, each nibble is a brilliant, full-bodied insight.

4. Diminished Food Squander and Maintainable Living:

Exact Ingredient Amounts: Dinner prepping in jar limits overabundance ingredients, lessening food squander and advancing a more supportable, eco-cognizant way of life.

Reusability of Jars: Using reusable glass bumps fundamentally eliminates single-use plastics, adding to a greener, all the more harmless to the ecosystem way to deal with feast planning.

5. Convenientce and Comfort:
In a hurry Prepared: Jars are a convenient, wreck free answer for those with occupied ways of life, guaranteeing that a nutritious meals is generally inside arm's range.
Ideal for Work or Travel: Whether at the workplace, on a climb, or on the way, a jostled meal gives an issue free, fulfilling choice.

6. Advances Careful Eating and Better Decisions:
Purposeful Dinner Arranging: The method involved with layering ingredients supports smart thought of every part's healthy benefit, advancing a more careful way to deal with eating.
Upholds Dietary Objectives: Meals Prepping in a jar enables people to adjust their dinners to explicit dietary prerequisites, whether for weight the board, wellness objectives, or exceptional dietary requirements.

7. Culinary Inventiveness and Various Menu Choices:

Unending Recipe Prospects: The container design takes into consideration a different cluster of culinary manifestations, from servings of mixed greens and grain bowls to soups, stews, and then some.

Worldwide Cooking Investigation: Try different things with many global flavors and ingredients, transforming each container into an identification to culinary undertakings.

All in all, the advantages of Meals Prepping in a jar reach out a long ways past simple comfort. It addresses a comprehensive way to deal with sustenance, using time productively, and supportability. By embracing this imaginative practice, people can enjoy the upsides of adjusted, delightful feasts while making progress towards a more careful, eco-cognizant way of life. This part is your passage to a culinary excursion that reclassifies the manner in which you approach dinner planning.

Choosing the Right Jars and Equipment

Embarking on the excursion of meals prepping in a jar is an undertaking that guarantees culinary comfort as well as a material for imaginative articulation. Notwithstanding, the selection of containers and going with gear assumes a pivotal part in guaranteeing the achievement and effectiveness of this undertaking. In this section, we will investigate the vital contemplations for choosing the right containers and hardware, directing you towards a consistent and compensating dinner preparing experience.

1. Jar Material and Size:

Glass versus Plastic: Selecting glass containers is energetically suggested, as they are non-receptive, safeguard enhances better, and are liberated from potential hurtful synthetic compounds that can filter into food. They are likewise more strong and simpler to clean than plastic partners.

Size Matters: Consider the part estimates you intend to get ready. More modest jars are great for individual servings, while bigger ones oblige heartier dinners.

2. Sealability and Impermeability:

Elastic Seals and Covers: Search for containers with elastic seals and secure covers to guarantee an impermeable conclusion. This component protects the freshness of ingredients as well as forestalls spills during transport.

3. Shape and Plan:

Straight-Sided versus Tightened: Straight-sided jars amplify extra room and work with simple stacking. Tightened containers, then again, offer an all the more tastefully satisfying show and might be ideal for specific kinds of dinners.

4. Simplicity of Cleaning and Upkeep:

Wide Mouth versus Standard Mouth: Wide-mouthed containers are more straightforward to clean and fill, particularly while layering ingredients. They likewise oblige bigger parts of food all the more without any problem.

5. Microwave and Cooler Similarity:

Microwave-Safe: Guarantee that the picked containers are microwave-safe, considering simple warming of feasts straightforwardly in the jar.

Freezer-Friendly: Search for jars that can endure frosty temperatures assuming you anticipate getting ready feasts ahead of time and putting away them in the cooler.

6. Solidness and Life span:
Thick Glass: Settle on jars produced using thick, durable glass to forestall breakage and guarantee life span, particularly assuming that you anticipate utilizing them routinely.

7. Correlative Gear:
Funnel: A pipe makes it simpler to layer fixings perfectly, particularly while working with more modest containers or accuracy layering.

Estimating Cups and Spoons: Exact estimations are critical to adjusted and flavorful dinners. Putting resources into quality estimating devices is a beneficial thought.

Naming Supplies: Names or markers are significant for taking note of the items and arrangement date of each jar.

8. Financial plan Contemplations:

Adjusting Quality and Cost: While top notch containers might be an underlying venture, they will generally be more strong and give better food safeguarding, at last contribution better worth over the long haul.

All in all, picking the right jars and equipment is a central stage towards an effective and charming involvement in feast preparing. Via cautiously thinking about elements like material, size, seal capacity, and corresponding instruments, you set up for a consistent and compensating culinary experience. This section fills in as your manual for going with informed choices that will upgrade your meal prepping journey.

Chapter 2: Breakfast Recipes in a jar

Classic Overnight Oats

Ingredients:
- 1/2 cup moved oats
- 1/2 cup milk (dairy or plant-based)
- 1 tablespoon chia seeds
- 1 tablespoon honey or maple syrup
- New berries and nuts for fixing

Preparation:
- In a jar, consolidate oats, milk, chia seeds, and sugar of decision.
- Mix well to guarantee even dissemination.

- Seal the jar and refrigerate for the time being.
- In the morning, give it a decent mix, add fixings, and appreciate!

Berry Blast Parfait

Ingredients:
- 1/2 cup Greek yogurt
- 1/4 cup granola
- 1/4 cup blended berries (strawberries, blueberries, raspberries)
- 1 tablespoon honey

Preparation:
- Start by layering Greek yogurt at the lower part of the jar.
- Add a layer of granola, trailed by a layer of blended berries.
- Sprinkle honey over the top.
- Rehash layers until the jar is filled.
- Seal and refrigerate until prepared to eat.

Veggie and Cheddar Omelet Jar

Ingredients:
- 2 eggs
- 2 tablespoons diced ringer peppers
- 2 tablespoons diced tomatoes
- 2 tablespoons diced onions
- 2 tablespoons destroyed cheddar
- Salt and pepper to taste

Preparation:
- Break eggs into the jar and beat them.
- Include the diced vegetables, cheddar, salt, and pepper.
- Screw the cover on firmly and shake until all ingredients are all around blended.
- Microwave for 2 minutes, blending part of the way through, until the omelet is completely cooked.

Chia Pudding Delight

Ingredients:
- 2 tablespoons chia seeds
- 1/2 cup milk (dairy or plant-based)
- 1 tablespoon honey or maple syrup
- 1/4 teaspoon vanilla concentrate

- Cut bananas and almonds for garnish

Preparation:
- In a jar, consolidate chia seeds, milk, sugar, and vanilla concentrate.
- Mix well and refrigerate for something like 2 hours or short-term.
- Mix again prior to garnish with banana cuts and almonds.

Mediterranean Quinoa Bowl

Ingredients:
- 1/2 cup cooked quinoa
- 2 tablespoons hummus
- 2 tablespoons diced cucumbers
- 2 tablespoons diced tomatoes
- 1 tablespoon disintegrated feta cheddar
- Kalamata olives for embellish

Preparation:
- Layer cooked quinoa at the lower part of the jar.
- Add hummus, trailed by diced cucumbers and tomatoes.
- Top with feta cheddar and enhancement with olives.
- Seal and refrigerate until prepared to eat.

Pesto and Tomato Breakfast Jar

Ingredients:
- 1/2 cup Greek yogurt
- 1 tablespoon basil pesto
- 2 tablespoons cherry tomatoes, split
- 1 tablespoon pine nuts

Preparation:
- Spoon Greek yogurt into the jar to make the main layer.
- Spread a layer of basil pesto on top of the yogurt.
- Add cherry tomatoes on top of the pesto layer.
- Sprinkle pine nuts for an additional crunch.
- Seal and refrigerate until prepared to appreciate.

Spinach and Feta Breakfast Jar

Ingredients:
- 2 eggs, beaten
- 1/4 cup cooked and cleaved spinach
- 2 tablespoons disintegrated feta cheddar
- 2 tablespoons cherry tomatoes, divided

Preparation:
- In a different bowl, whisk the eggs and put away.
- Start by layering half of the beaten eggs at the lower part of the container.
- Add a layer of cooked spinach, trailed by a layer of feta cheddar and cherry tomatoes.
- Pour the leftover beaten eggs on top.
- Seal the container and refrigerate.
- At the point when prepared to eat, microwave for 2-3 minutes, mixing part of the way through, until the eggs are completely cooked.

Banana Nut Overnight Oats

Ingredients:
- 1/2 cup moved oats
- 1/2 cup milk (dairy or plant-based)
- 1 ready banana, squashed
- 2 tablespoons cleaved nuts (e.g., pecans, almonds)
- 1 tablespoon honey

Preparation:
- In a jar, consolidate moved oats, milk, and squashed banana.

- Mix well to completely blend all ingredients.
- Top with hacked nuts and shower honey for pleasantness.
- Seal the container and refrigerate for the time being.

Avocado and Egg Breakfast Jar

Ingredients:
- 1/2 avocado, diced
- 2 eggs, hard-bubbled and cut
- 2 tablespoons cherry tomatoes, split
- 1 tablespoon disintegrated feta cheddar

Preparation:
- Begin with a layer of diced avocado at the lower part of the jar.
- Add the cut hard-bubbled eggs on top of the avocado.
- Place divided cherry tomatoes around the eggs.
- Sprinkle disintegrated feta cheddar over the top.
- Seal and refrigerate until prepared to appreciate.

Peanut Butter and Banana Chia Pudding

Ingredients:
- 2 tablespoons chia seeds
- 1/2 cup milk (dairy or plant-based)
- 2 tablespoons peanut butter
- 1 ready banana, cut

Preparation:
- In a jar, consolidate chia seeds, milk, and peanut butter.
- Mix well to guarantee even conveyance.
- Refrigerate for something like 2 hours or short-term.
- Top with cut bananas prior to serving.

Chapter 3: Snacks and Sweets in Jars

Trail Blend Energy Chomps

Ingredients:
- 1/2 cup moved oats
- 1/4 cup peanut butter
- 1/4 cup honey
- 1/4 cup hacked nuts (e.g., almonds, cashews)
- 2 tablespoons dried natural products (e.g., cranberries, raisins)

- 2 tablespoons chocolate chips

Preparation:
- In a blending bowl, consolidate moved oats, peanut butter, and honey.
- Add hacked nuts, dried natural products, and chocolate chips. Blend well.
- Scoop spoonfuls of the combination into little jar.
- Press the blend down to make conservative nibbles.
- Refrigerate for no less than 30 minutes prior to fixing the jar.

Layered Greek Yogurt Parfait

Ingredients:
- 1/2 cup Greek yogurt
- 2 tablespoons honey or maple syrup
- 2 tablespoons granola
- 2 tablespoons blended berries (e.g., strawberries, blueberries)
- 1 tablespoon slashed nuts (e.g., pecans, walnuts)

Preparation:
- Start with a layer of Greek yogurt at the lower part of the jar.

- Shower honey or maple syrup over the yogurt.
- Add a layer of granola, trailed by blended berries.
- Sprinkle slashed nuts on top.
- Seal and refrigerate until prepared to enjoy.

Apple Cinnamon Biscuit Jar

Ingredients:
- 1/2 cup moved oats
- 1/2 cup milk (dairy or plant-based)
- 1/4 cup unsweetened fruit purée
- 1 tablespoon honey
- 1/2 teaspoon cinnamon
- 1/4 teaspoon vanilla concentrate
- Slashed apples and a sprinkle of cinnamon for fixing

Preparation:
- In a jar, join moved oats, milk, fruit purée, honey, cinnamon, and vanilla concentrate.
- Mix well to guarantee all ingredients are blended completely.
- Top with hacked apples and an additional sprinkle of cinnamon.
- Seal and refrigerate overnight.

No-Heat Chocolate Cheesecake

Ingredients:
- 1/4 cup chocolate treat scraps
- 1/4 cup cream cheddar
- 2 tablespoons powdered sugar
- 2 tablespoons cocoa powder
- Whipped cream and chocolate shavings for garnish

Ingredients:
- Begin with a layer of chocolate treat morsels at the lower part of the jar.
- In a different bowl, blend cream cheddar, powdered sugar, and cocoa powder until smooth.
- Spoon the cream cheddar blend over the treat pieces.
- Top with a bit of whipped cream and chocolate shavings.
- Seal and refrigerate until prepared to enjoy.

Mango Coconut Chia Pudding

Ingredients:
- 2 tablespoons chia seeds
- 1/2 cup coconut milk
- 1/4 cup diced mango
- 1 tablespoon destroyed coconut

Preparation:
- In a jar, join chia seeds and coconut milk.
- Mix well and refrigerate for no less than 2 hours or short-term.
- Layer diced mango on top and sprinkle with destroyed coconut.

Chocolate Peanut Butter Delight

Ingredients:
- 1/4 cup chocolate granola
- 1/4 cup Greek yogurt
- 1 tablespoon peanut butter
- 1 tablespoon chocolate chips

Preparation:
- Start with a layer of chocolate granola at the lower part of the jar.
- Add a layer of Greek yogurt on top.
- Shower peanut butter over the yogurt.

- Sprinkle chocolate chips for an additional treat.
- Seal and refrigerate until prepared to enjoy.

Lemon Blueberry Cheesecake Parfait

Ingredients:
- 1/2 cup Greek yogurt
- 2 tablespoons lemon curd
- 2 tablespoons blueberries (new or frozen)
- 2 tablespoons granola

Ingredients:
- Begin with a layer of Greek yogurt at the lower part of the jar.
- Add a layer of lemon curd on top.
- Add a layer of blueberries and a sprinkle of granola.
- Rehash layers until the jar is filled.
- Seal and refrigerate until prepared to enjoy.

Almond Satisfaction Chia Pudding

Ingredients:
- 2 tablespoons chia seeds

- 1/2 cup almond milk
- 1 tablespoon cocoa powder
- 1 tablespoon destroyed coconut
- Cut almonds and chocolate chips for fixing

Preparation:
- In a jar, consolidate chia seeds, almond milk, cocoa powder, and destroyed coconut.
- Mix well and refrigerate for something like 2 hours or short-term.
- Top with cut almonds and chocolate chips prior to serving.

Caramel Fruity dessert Short-term Oats

Ingredients:
- 1/2 cup moved oats
- 1/2 cup milk (dairy or plant-based)
- 2 tablespoons unsweetened fruit purée
- 1 tablespoon caramel sauce
- Slashed apples and a sprinkle of cinnamon for garnish

Preparation:
- In a jar, join moved oats, milk, fruit purée, and caramel sauce.
- Mix well to guarantee all ingredients are blended completely.

- Top with cleaved apples and a sprinkle of cinnamon.
- Seal and refrigerate for the time being.

Banana Split Breakfast Jar

Ingredients:
- 1/2 cup Greek yogurt
- 2 tablespoons chocolate chips
- 2 tablespoons cut bananas
- 1 tablespoon cleaved nuts (e.g., pecans, peanuts)
- Whipped cream and a maraschino cherry for garnish

Preparation:
- Start with a layer of Greek yogurt at the lower part of the jar.
- Add a layer of chocolate chips, trailed by cut bananas and hacked nuts.
- Top with a touch of whipped cream and a maraschino cherry.
- Seal and refrigerate until prepared to enjoy.

Chapter 4: Main course mix in a jar

Mexican Enchilada Goulash

Ingredients:
- 1/2 cup cooked dark beans
- 1/2 cup cooked corn parts
- 1/4 cup diced ringer peppers
- 1/4 cup diced onions
- 1/4 cup destroyed cheddar
- 2 tablespoons enchilada sauce

Preparation:
- Layer cooked dark beans at the lower part of the jar.

- Add cooked corn, diced chime peppers, and diced onions.
- Sprinkle destroyed cheddar over the top.
- Pour enchilada sauce over the ingredients.
- Seal and refrigerate until prepared to utilize. To cook, move to a microwave-safe dish and intensity until warmed through.

Baked Ziti with Sausage

Ingredients:
- 1/2 cup cooked ziti pasta
- 1/4 cup cooked and disintegrated Italian frankfurter
- 1/4 cup marinara sauce
- 1/4 cup destroyed mozzarella cheddar
- 1 tablespoon ground Parmesan cheddar

Preparation:
- Begin with a layer of cooked ziti pasta at the lower part of the jar.
- Add cooked and disintegrated Italian hotdog.
- Pour marinara sauce over the ingredients.
- Sprinkle destroyed mozzarella and ground Parmesan cheddar on top.

- Seal and refrigerate until prepared to utilize. To cook, move to a stove safe dish and heat until cheddar is effervescent and brilliant.

Yam and Dark Bean Bake

Ingredients:
- 1/2 cup cooked yam shapes
- 1/2 cup cooked dark beans
- 1/4 cup diced ringer peppers
- 1/4 cup diced red onions
- 1/4 cup destroyed Monterey Jack cheddar
- 1 tablespoon olive oil

Preparation:
- Start with a layer of cooked yam 3D squares at the lower part of the jar.
- Add cooked dark beans, diced chime peppers, and diced red onions.
- Shower olive oil over the ingredients.
- Sprinkle destroyed Monterey Jack cheddar on top.
- Seal and refrigerate until prepared to utilize. To cook, move to a stove safe dish and prepare until warmed through.

Chicken and Broccoli Alfredo

Ingredients:
- 1/2 cup cooked chicken bosom, diced
- 1/2 cup cooked broccoli florets
- 1/4 cup Alfredo sauce
- 1/4 cup cooked fettuccine pasta
- 1 tablespoon ground Parmesan cheddar

Preparation:
- Start with a layer of diced cooked chicken bosom at the lower part of the jar.
- Add cooked broccoli florets and cooked fettuccine pasta.
- Pour Alfredo sauce over the ingredients.
- Sprinkle ground Parmesan cheddar on top.
- Seal and refrigerate until prepared to utilize. To cook, move to a stove safe dish and prepare until warmed through.

Eggplant Parmesan

Ingredients:
- 1/2 cup cooked eggplant cuts
- 1/4 cup marinara sauce
- 1/4 cup destroyed mozzarella cheddar
- 2 tablespoons ground Parmesan cheddar

- 1 tablespoon olive oil

Preparation:
- Begin with a layer of cooked eggplant cuts at the lower part of the jar.
- Pour marinara sauce over the eggplant.
- Sprinkle destroyed mozzarella and ground Parmesan cheddar on top.
- Shower olive oil over the ingredients.
- Seal and refrigerate until prepared to utilize. To cook, move to a stove safe dish and heat until cheddar is effervescent and brilliant.

Teriyaki Salmon with Brown Rice

Ingredients:
- 1/2 cup cooked salmon, chipped
- 1/4 cup teriyaki sauce
- 1/2 cup cooked earthy colored rice
- 2 tablespoons cut green onions

Preparation:
- Begin with a layer of cooked, chipped salmon at the lower part of the jar.
- Poured teriyaki sauce over the salmon.
- Add a layer of cooked earthy colored rice on top of the sauce.
- Sprinkle cut green onions as a trimming.

- Seal and refrigerate until prepared to utilize. To serve, microwave until warmed through.

Spinach and Feta Stuffed Ringer Peppers

Ingredients:
- 1/2 cup cooked quinoa
- 1/4 cup cooked spinach
- 2 tablespoons disintegrated feta cheddar
- 2 tablespoons diced tomatoes
- 2 chime peppers

Preparation:
- Blend cooked quinoa, spinach, feta cheddar, and diced tomatoes in a bowl.
- Remove the tops the ringer peppers and eliminate seeds and layers.
- Stuff the peppers with the quinoa combination.
- Place the stuffed peppers in the container.
- Seal and refrigerate until prepared to utilize. To cook, move to a broiler safe dish and prepare until peppers are delicate.

Lemon Garlic Shrimp and Orzo

Ingredients:
- 1/2 cup cooked shrimp
- 1/4 cup lemon garlic sauce
- 1/2 cup cooked orzo pasta
- 1 tablespoon cleaved parsley

Preparation:
- Begin with a layer of cooked shrimp at the lower part of the jar.
- Pour lemon garlic sauce over the shrimp.
- Add a layer of cooked orzo pasta on top of the sauce.
- Sprinkle slashed parsley as an embellishment.
- Seal and refrigerate until prepared to utilize. To serve, microwave until warmed through.

Pesto Chicken with Sun-Dried Tomatoes

Ingredients:
- 1/2 cup cooked chicken bosom, diced
- 2 tablespoons basil pesto
- 2 tablespoons sun-dried tomatoes, slashed
- 1/2 cup cooked penne pasta

Preparation:
- Begin with a layer of diced cooked chicken bosom at the lower part of the jar.
- Spread basil pesto over the chicken.
- Add cleaved sun-dried tomatoes on top of the pesto. Layer with cooked penne pasta.
- Seal and refrigerate until prepared to utilize. To serve, microwave until warmed through.

Meat and Grain Stew

Ingredients:
- 1/2 cup cooked meat pieces
- 1/4 cup diced carrots
- 1/4 cup diced celery
- 1/4 cup cooked grain
- 1/2 cup meat stock, 2 tablespoons diced tomatoes

Preparation:
- Begin with a layer of cooked meat lumps at the lower part of the jar.
- Add diced carrots and celery.
- Layer with cooked grain.
- Pour hamburger stock over the fixings.
- Top with diced tomatoes. Seal and refrigerate until prepared to utilize. To serve, microwave until warmed through.

Chapter 5: Soup and sauce mix in a jar

Classic Tomato Soup

Ingredients:
- 1/4 cup dried tomato soup blend
- 2 tablespoons dried basil leaves
- 1 tablespoon dried minced onions
- 1 tablespoon dried parsley pieces

Preparation:
- In a jar, layer the dried tomato soup blend, dried basil, dried minced onions, and dried parsley pieces.
- Seal the jar and store in a cool, dry spot.
- To make soup, consolidate the items in the container with high temp water and cook as per bundle directions.

Rich Mushroom Sauce

Ingredients:
- 1/4 cup dried mushroom soup blend
- 2 tablespoons dried thyme leaves
- 1 tablespoon dried minced garlic
- 1 tablespoon dried chives

Preparation:
- In a jar, layer the dried mushroom soup blend, dried thyme, dried minced garlic, and dried chives.
- Seal the jar and store in a cool, dry spot.
- To make the sauce, consolidate the items in the container with high temp water and cook as per bundle guidelines.

Zesty Lentil Soup

Ingredients:
- 1/4 cup dried lentil soup blend
- 2 tablespoons dried cumin
- 1 tablespoon dried bean stew pieces
- 1 tablespoon dried coriander

Preparation:
- In a jar, layer the dried lentil soup blend, dried cumin, dried bean stew drops, and dried coriander.
- Seal the jar and store in a cool, dry spot.
- To make soup, join the items in the container with boiling water and cook as per bundle directions.

Velvety Garlic Parmesan Sauce

Ingredients:
- 1/4 cup dried garlic parmesan sauce blend
- 2 tablespoons dried basil leaves
- 1 tablespoon dried minced garlic
- 1 tablespoon dried parsley chips

Preparation:

- In a jar, layer the dried garlic parmesan sauce blend, dried basil, dried minced garlic, and dried parsley chips.
- Seal the jar and store in a cool, dry spot.
- To make the sauce, consolidate the items in the container with boiling water and cook as per bundle directions.

Moroccan Chickpea Soup

Ingredients:
- 1/4 cup dried chickpea soup blend
- 2 tablespoons ground cumin
- 1 tablespoon ground coriander
- 1 tablespoon ground turmeric

Preparation:
- In a jar, layer the dried chickpea soup blend, ground cumin, ground coriander, and ground turmeric.
- Seal the jar and store in a cool, dry spot.
- To make soup, consolidate the items in the container with heated water and cook as per bundle guidelines.

Smooth Alfredo Sauce

Ingredients:
- 1/4 cup dried alfredo sauce blend
- 2 tablespoons dried thyme leaves
- 1 tablespoon dried minced garlic
- 1 tablespoon dried parsley drops

Preparation:
- In a jar, layer the dried alfredo sauce blend, dried thyme, dried minced garlic, and dried parsley drops.
- Seal the jar and store in a cool, dry spot.
- To make the sauce, join the items in the container with boiling water and cook as per bundle guidelines.

Thai Coconut Curry Soup

Ingredients:
- 1/4 cup dried coconut curry soup blend
- 2 tablespoons dried ginger
- 1 tablespoon dried lemongrass
- 1 tablespoon dried red bean stew drops

Preparation:

- In a jar, layer the dried coconut curry soup blend, dried ginger, dried lemongrass, and dried red bean stew pieces.
- Seal the jar and store in a cool, dry spot.
- To make soup, join the items in the container with high temp water and cook as per bundle directions.

Rich Wild Mushroom Sauce

Ingredients:
- 1/4 cup dried wild mushroom sauce blend
- 2 tablespoons dried thyme leaves
- 1 tablespoon dried minced garlic
- 1 tablespoon dried chives

Preparation:
- In a jar, layer the dried wild mushroom sauce blend, dried thyme, dried minced garlic, and dried chives.
- Seal the jar and store in a cool, dry spot.
- To make the sauce, join the items in the container with high temp water and cook as per bundle guidelines.

Part Pea and Ham Soup

Ingredients:
- 1/4 cup dried split pea soup blend
- 2 tablespoons dried thyme leaves
- 1 tablespoon dried minced onions
- 1 tablespoon dried parsley chips

Preparation:
- In a jar, layer the dried split pea soup blend, dried thyme, dried minced onions, and dried parsley drops.
- Seal the jar and store in a cool, dry spot.
- To make soup, consolidate the items in the container with heated water and cook as per bundle directions.

Sun-Dried Tomato Pesto Sauce

Ingredients:
- 1/4 cup dried sun-dried tomato pesto sauce blend
- 2 tablespoons dried basil leaves
- 1 tablespoon dried minced garlic
- 1 tablespoon dried oregano

Preparation:
- In a jar, layer the dried sun-dried tomato pesto sauce blend, dried basil, dried minced garlic, and dried oregano.
- Seal the jar and store in a cool, dry spot.
- To make the sauce, consolidate the items in the jar with boiling water and cook as per bundle guidelines.

Chapter 6: Rice mix in a jar

Mexican Rice Mix

Ingredients:
- 1 cup long-grain white rice
- 2 tablespoons bean stew powder
- 1 tablespoon ground cumin
- 1 tablespoon dried oregano
- 1 teaspoon salt

Preparation:
- In a jar, layer the rice followed by bean stew powder, ground cumin, dried oregano, and salt.
- Seal the jar and store in a cool, dry spot.
- To cook, join the items in the container with 2 cups of water in a pot. Heat to the point of boiling, then diminish intensity and stew until rice is delicate.

Lemon Spice Rice Mix

Ingredients:
- 1 cup long-grain white rice
- 2 tablespoons dried parsley chips
- 1 tablespoon dried thyme leaves
- 1 tablespoon lemon zing
- 1 teaspoon salt

Preparation:
- In a jar, layer the rice followed by dried parsley, dried thyme, lemon zing, and salt.
- Seal the jar and store in a cool, dry spot.
- To cook, consolidate the items in the container with 2 cups of water in a pot. Heat to the point of boiling, then, at that point, lessen intensity and stew until rice is delicate.

Coconut Curry Rice Mix

Ingredients:
- 1 cup long-grain white rice
- 2 tablespoons curry powder
- 1/4 cup dried coconut drops
- 1 teaspoon salt

Preparation:
- In a jar, layer the rice followed by curry powder, dried coconut pieces, and salt.
- Seal the jar and store in a cool, dry spot.
- To cook, join the items in the jar with 2 cups of water and 1/2 cup coconut milk in a pot. Heat to the point of boiling, then, at that point, diminish intensity and stew until rice is delicate.

Spanish Rice Mix

Ingredients:
- 1 cup long-grain white rice
- 2 tablespoons stew powder
- 1 tablespoon ground cumin
- 1 tablespoon dried oregano
- 1 teaspoon smoked paprika
- 1 teaspoon salt

Preparation:
- In a jar, layer the rice followed by bean stew powder, ground cumin, dried oregano, smoked paprika, and salt.
- Seal the jar and store in a cool, dry spot.
- To cook, join the items in the jar with 2 cups of pureed tomatoes in a pan. Heat to the point of boiling, then, at that point, diminish intensity and stew until rice is delicate.

Herbed Wild Rice Mix

Ingredients:
- 1 cup wild rice
- 2 tablespoons dried thyme leaves
- 1 tablespoon dried rosemary leaves
- 1 tablespoon dried sage leaves
- 1 teaspoon salt

Preparation:
- In a jar, layer the wild rice followed by dried thyme, dried rosemary, dried sage, and salt.
- Seal the jar and store in a cool, dry spot.
- To cook, join the items in the container with 2 1/2 cups of water in a pot. Heat to the point of boiling, then diminish intensity and stew until rice is delicate.

Garlic Parmesan Rice Mix

Ingredients:
- 1 cup long-grain white rice
- 2 tablespoons dried minced garlic
- 1/4 cup ground Parmesan cheddar
- 1 teaspoon salt

Preparation:
- In a jar, layer the rice followed by dried minced garlic, ground Parmesan cheddar, and salt.
- Seal the jar and store in a cool, dry spot.
- To cook, join the items in the container with 2 cups of chicken or vegetable stock in a pot. Heat to the point of boiling, then, at that point, diminish intensity and stew until rice is delicate.

Thai Pineapple Broiled Rice Mix

Ingredients:
- 1 cup jasmine rice
- 2 tablespoons curry powder
- 1/4 cup dried pineapple pieces
- 1/4 cup cashews
- 1 teaspoon salt

Preparation:
- In a jar, layer the jasmine rice followed by curry powder, dried pineapple pieces, cashews, and salt.
- Seal the jar and store in a cool, dry spot.
- To cook, join the items in the jar with 2 cups of water in a pan. Heat to the point of boiling, then decrease intensity and stew until rice is delicate. Cushion with a fork and serve.

Mushroom Risotto Mix

Ingredients:
- 1 cup Arborio rice
- 2 tablespoons dried minced onions
- 1/4 cup dried mushrooms
- 1/4 cup ground Parmesan cheddar
- 1 teaspoon salt

Preparation:
- In a jar, layer the Arborio rice followed by dried minced onions, dried mushrooms, ground Parmesan cheddar, and salt.
- Seal the jar and store in a cool, dry spot.
- To cook, consolidate the items in the container with 4 cups of chicken or vegetable stock in a pan.

- Heat to the point of boiling, then diminish intensity and stew until rice is velvety and delicate.

Lemon Asparagus Rice Mix

Ingredients:
- 1 cup long-grain white rice
- 2 tablespoons dried lemon zing
- 1/4 cup dried asparagus pieces
- 1 teaspoon salt

Preparation:
- In a jar, layer the rice followed by dried lemon zing, dried asparagus pieces, and salt.
- Seal the jar and store in a cool, dry spot.
- To cook, join the items in the jar with 2 cups of water in a pot. Heat to the point of boiling, then diminish intensity and stew until rice is delicate.

Mediterranean Couscous Mix

Ingredients:
- 1 cup couscous
- 2 tablespoons dried sun-dried tomatoes
- 2 tablespoons dried basil leaves
- 2 tablespoons dried oregano

- 1 teaspoon salt

Preparation:
- In a jar, layer the couscous followed by dried sun-dried tomatoes, dried basil, dried oregano, and salt.
- Seal the jar and store in a cool, dry spot.
- To cook, consolidate the items in the container with 1 1/4 cups of bubbling water in a heatproof bowl. Cover and let sit for 5 minutes, then cushion with a fork.

Chapter 7: Expert Tips for Storing and Reheating Meals

Proficiently putting away and warming jostled feasts is pivotal to guarantee that they stay new, tasty, and protected to consume. Here are a few master tips to assist you with becoming the best at dinner capacity and warming:

1. Pick the Right Jars:
Pick top caliber, sealed shut jars made of materials like glass or without bpa plastic. These materials assist with keeping up with the newness of your feasts and forestall any expected spillage.

2. Name and Date Your Jars:
Naming your jars with the items and date of arrangement is fundamental for monitoring newness. Utilize waterproof names or a marker intended for use on containers.

3. Follow Legitimate Layering Strategies:
While getting ready mix in-a-jars recipes, guarantee that ingredients are layered in a calculated way.

For instance, putting wet ingredients like sauces or dressings at the base can keep the dry ingredients from becoming spongy.

4. Keep Wet and Dry Ingredients Discrete:
While putting away servings of mixed greens or dishes with both wet and dry parts, think about utilizing separate compartments inside the jar, similar to a divider or extra more modest holders.

5. Take into account Satisfactory Head Space:
Leave a space at the highest point of the jar to consider extension during freezing or refrigeration. This keeps jars from breaking.

6. Refrigerate or Freeze Speedily:
Subsequent to setting up your bumped feasts, refrigerate or freeze them instantly to keep up with their quality. The speedier they cool down, the better they'll keep.

7. Practice Safe Warming Strategies:
Continuously warm your jolted meals to the fitting interior temperature to guarantee they are protected to eat. Utilize a food thermometer to check for doneness.

8. Change Cooking Times and Temperatures:
Contingent upon the kind of meals, change the warming time and temperature likewise. For instance, soups might require gentler warming than strong dishes.

9. Use Microwave-Safe Tops or Covers:
While warming in the microwave, guarantee that the top or cover is microwave-safe. This forestalls any expected harm to the holder or seal.

10. Consider Ventilation During Warming:
While utilizing a microwave, pass on a little hole for ventilation to forestall pressure development. This serves to equally warm the feast and maintains a strategic distance from likely spills or mishaps.

11. Mix and Check for Consistency:
Blending the items in the container during warming can assist with disseminating heat uniformly and guarantee reliable outcomes. Check for the ideal temperature and surface in the interim.

12. Screen Surface and Taste:
Focus on the surface and taste of your warmed feast. Change cooking times or strategies on a case by case basis to accomplish the ideal result.

13. Try not to Warm Specific Ingredients:
A few ingredients, as sensitive spices or new greens, are best added in the wake of warming to safeguard their flavor and surface.

Customizing Recipes to Suit Your Tastes

One of the best delights of cooking is the chance to put your own touch on a dish. In the "Meals in a Jar Cookbook," we've given various tasty recipes as a beginning stage, however don't hesitate for even a moment to get imaginative and make them your own. Here are a few master tips on the best way to modify recipes to suit your exceptional preferences:

1. Change Flavors and Flavors:
Try different things with various spices, flavors, and flavors to add your number one flavors.
Whether you favor some additional garlic or a bit of intensity, preparing changes can change a dish.

2. Play with Ingredient Proportions:
Go ahead and change ingredient extents to match your inclinations. To eliminate a specific fixing, feel free to conform however you would prefer.

3. Trade Protein Sources:
Substitute proteins in view of your dietary inclinations or what's accessible. For instance, supplant chicken with tofu, or trade hamburger for mushrooms for a veggie lover turn.

4. Customize Surface and Consistency:
Change the surface of a dish however you would prefer. Mix elements for a smoother consistency or leave them chunkier for added surface. This can altogether influence the general insight of the meal.

5. Explore different avenues regarding Flavors and Sauces:
Feel free to change around sauces and flavor profiles. For example, you can attempt an alternate sort of marinade or trade a tomato-based sauce for a velvety one.

6. Consolidate Ethnic Flavors:
Imbue recipes with the kinds of various foods from around the world. Whether it's adding soy sauce for an Asian curve or involving cumin and coriander for a dash of Indian food, investigating various flavors can really rouse.

7. Customize with Ingredients and Enhancements:
Ingredients and embellishments offer a valuable chance to add a final detail. Sprinkle with new spices, add a shower of sauce, or top with some crunchy nuts or seeds for added surface and flavor.

8. Change Pleasantness and Acridity:
Calibrate the equilibrium of prepared components in recipes like sauces or dressings. This permits you to make a flavor profile that suits your sense of taste impeccably.

9. Investigate Elective Ingredients:
Be available to utilizing elective ingredients in light of dietary necessities or inclinations. For example, substitute dairy with plant-based choices or attempt sans gluten options.

10. Make it Your Own Particular Dish:
As you become more familiar with modifying recipes, you might find that specific dishes become your particular manifestations. These are recipes that mirror your remarkable taste and style.

CONCLUSION

In the "Meals in a Jar Cookbook," we've set out on a culinary excursion that joins comfort, flavor, and imagination to make preparing a feast a wonderful and proficient experience. Through the pages of this book, we've investigated a different scope of recipes that can be ready, put away, and delighted in directly from a jar.

This cookbook has been intended to improve your meal planning, whether you're getting ready for breakfast, lunch, supper, snacks, soups, sauces, or sweets. Every recipe gives a complete aide on the most proficient method to make these delightful, outwardly engaging, and healthfully adjusted jolted meals.

By picking the right Jars and equipment, we've guaranteed that your meals stay new and tempting. We've examined the significance of water/air proof seals, measuring, and marks, all of which add to a fruitful dinner preparation experience. In the domain of breakfast recipes, we've found how to make morning delights that can be appreciated in a hurry.

From granola parfaits to expedite oats, these recipes offer a flavorful and nutritious beginning to your day. For main courses, we've revealed a universe of flavors, from Mexican Enchilada Goulash to Lemon Garlic Shrimp and Orzo. The adaptability of mix in-a-jar recipes permits you to adjust and fit dishes as you would prefer and dietary inclinations.

Soups and sauces have not been neglected, offering choices for ameliorating and delightful meals that can be immediately ready. Whether you're in the state of mind for an exemplary tomato soup or a rich mushroom sauce, the conceivable outcomes are huge. Also, we should not fail to remember the sweet joys. Our sweet mix in-a-jar recipes range from exemplary chocolate chip treats to colorful s'mores brownies, giving a superb end to any feast.

In conclusion, the "Meals in a Jar Cookbook" enables you to smooth out your meal prepping process while guaranteeing that you never think twice about taste or quality. An asset offers flavorful recipes as well as the comfort of having feasts prepared when you want them. As you embark on your excursion into the universe of bumped feasts, recollect that trial and error is supported.

Don't hesitate for even a moment to blend and match fixings, adjust recipes to your inclinations, and make each jostled feast genuinely your own.

We trust this cookbook has roused you to investigate the craft of meal prepping in a jar and to find the delight of speedy, advantageous, and tasty feasting encounters. With these recipes and strategies in your culinary toolbox, the potential outcomes are huge, and each dinner can turn into a tasty experience. Partake in your excursion into the universe of jolted dinners, and may it bring you both culinary fulfillment and valuable time saved in the kitchen.

Blissful prepping and more joyful feasting!

Made in the USA
Monee, IL
13 February 2024